When They Come For You

The Frogmore Press

ISBN 978 0 9531383 6 4

First published by
The Frogmore Press
21 Mildmay Road
Lewes
East Sussex
BN7 1PJ

www.frogmorepress.co.uk

This edition published in 2011

Printed by Hythe Printers, Pennypot Estate, Hythe, Kent
CT21 6PE

A catalogue record for this book is available from the British Library

Cover design by Neil Gower

Michael Swan

When They Come For You

For Katy

Acknowledgements

This collection includes poems which have appeared in *The Frogmore Papers, The Times Literary Supplement, Poetry Life, The Arts Club Journal, Isthmus, Envoi,* the Lancaster Litfest anthologies and elsewhere. My thanks to the editors concerned for the hospitality of their pages.

My thanks, also, to the people (too many to name) who have helped me with encouragement, advice and criticism over the years, and who must accept a share of the responsibility for what follows.

Contents

SANTA MARIA DEL MAR

At the entrance to the church
we are warned
to beware of flower sellers.

I will not beware of flower sellers.

I know enough already
to beware of burglars,
soldiers,
relatives,
education authorities,
consultants,
publishers,
and all governments.

But flower-sellers!

I will not.
Nor will I beware
of poets,
the mothers of small children,
students of philosophy,
tired waitresses,
people buying their first car,
the makers of walking sticks,
or old ladies
counting their change slowly in the supermarket.

I will not lose
my last crumbs of trust.

And if tomorrow
I am robbed by a flower seller
it will be a small price to pay.

GOD GETS EFFICIENT

God has set up
a Customer Services Department.
This has revolutionised
communications with the Divine Essence.
Only last week
I had a letter
acknowledging my recent prayers
for spiritual counsel / help in time of trouble / a speedy recovery
(delete where inapplicable),
which would be given the fullest consideration;
also a note
addressed to a Ms Postlethwaite
enclosing a Heavenly cashcard;
an apology
for any inconvenience
caused by the Flood;
and a document
sent by special delivery
notifying me of my impending birth.

FAIR COPY

The fact is,
God spoke lousy Hebrew
and Moses was going deaf.

He got the strange gods one OK
– that was bloody typical –
but the rest ...

Something about not convicting poultry?
Don't cover your neighbour's roof
or force biscuits against him?
Thou shalt not spill something.
Steel?
Remember the cat's away, to keep it rolling?

Never mind, he thought.
I'll dream something up,
keep the buggers in order.

CARLOTTI

Do you remember?
We met in Bologna
where Carlotti gave that wonderful talk.
I was wearing my blue
and James was being difficult
because of Melanie.
Carlotti: such a *distinguished* mind.
The weather was just perfect,
wasn't it?
Bright, but not too warm,
and there's something about Bologna,
all those colonnades
if that's the right word.
Carlotti: he really makes one question
all one's basic beliefs.
We found an amazing restaurant –
that's the thing about Bologna,
you're hungry,
you just walk into the nearest restaurant
and you're sure of a fabulous meal.
Carlotti: it's a matter of presence
as much as anything.
And that Italian stationery
£1 a sheet
and you'd never write on it
but just, somehow,
inexpressibly exquisite.
I ended up in bed
with a man I met on the way out.
Not like me at all,
but it just felt *right*
if you know what I mean.
Carlotti: it was a real *privilege* to listen to him.
We went up to the monastery
in the afternoon
and Jake got mugged
by a couple of teenagers
but they only got £20
and an out-of-date visa card.

Carlotti: you're just not the same person afterwards,
you know.
And I saw this trouser suit ...

FOR THE PIANIST IN THE CONRAD HOTEL, ISTANBUL, 25.5.02

Two minutes only,
and I had to leave
for less important things.
But you were astounding.
Technique, beauty,
as much as anyone could wish,
but something more.
Your whole life
was there in your playing.

I heard
how you came from a poor family
in Eastern Anatolia;
how you worked
for a slave-driving farmer,
wore yourself out,
but after work
practised into the night;
how you went short of food,
clothes, shoes even,
sacrificed everything
for your music.

Your playing told me
(as you transposed into the minor)
how once you broke your arm,
and thought
you would never play again.
But an old school friend
who studied medicine
performed miracles.

In a dance of arpeggios,
I learnt how you fell in love
with a young nurse
called Fatima,
and how your fortune turned.

You found a well-paid job
in a hotel,
playing amazing
heart-breaking music
for rich people who don't listen.

In the evening
(I heard in a series of glissandos)
you go home, late,
to your wife,
who is as beautiful
as the day when you met;
to your two children
(who you hope will have easier lives),
and to the dog,
whom you rescued from the street,
and who is not musical at all.

Well,
I may be wrong
about some of the details.
But I loved your playing.

HALFWAY TO ETERNITY

In a good hotel
on his fortieth birthday,
he nurses a hangover
and sips his coffee.

Five hours' walk
above the valley
there are gentians and saxifrage,
and a stream falling.

He brushes his teeth,
collects his papers,
and takes a cab
to the first meeting.

Below the pass,
snow finches
flash and whirl
across the scree.

Half the board
are ready to sign,
but he can't convince
the fund managers.

Chamois move up
into the cirque;
reach the ridge
and disappear.

He takes a break
and inspects the plant,
nodding and smiling
round the shop floor.

Above the moraine
four elements:
snow, sun,
rock and ice.

The accountants are evasive.
He has lunch
with a woman from marketing,
nearly calls his wife.

A snow slope
leads up to a cornice.
Some tricky scrambling,
then out at the top.

Afternoon fades
into evening drizzle.
They finish haggling.
He phones London.

Another hour
fighting the wind;
one last crevasse
and the summit rocks.

Back in a cab
past the bus queues.
A bath; then dinner
with a good bottle.

Here, now,
is the top of the world,
the sky vast,
halfway to eternity.

He falls asleep
watching a film
about three lesbians,
on his fortieth birthday.

HOW WOULD I KNOW?

I saw her walking barefoot
in the rain.

Back from her lover's arms
returning home.

Or driven by a quarrel
yet again.

Waiting to die,
and have an end of pain.

Or simply happy
once to be alone,
to feel the water running
on her skin.

How would I know?

I saw her walking barefoot
in the rain.

MY NEIGHBOUR

My neighbour
has large capable hands,
an open friendly face,
and a ready smile.

He can change a fanbelt,
build a treehouse,
set a sail,
keep goal,
chair a committee,
drink with the boys,
and sing 'Eskimo Nell'.

I can do none of these things.

Perhaps my neighbour lies awake
wishing he could draft an abstract,
translate an epigram,
trace an etymology,
or write a villanelle.

But I doubt it.

WE TRIED TO TELL YOU

In a shabby pub
down a back street
late one evening,
I found my old maths master
sitting at a corner table,
crying.

Not a pretty sight,
an old maths teacher
weeping into his beer.

'Let me tell you this,'
he said.
'It does not add up.
It does not fucking add up.

Two plus two
is a random number.

The angles of a triangle
sum to 37 degrees, or 460, or minus 11,
or nothing you can determine.
Circles bulge.
Squares don't have enough corners.
Parallel lines
all meet
or do not exist
or go where they bloody feel like.
The x axis
does not come on the same page
as the y axis.

There is no geometry
that fits our space.

You get on the number 4 bus for the station,
and when you arrive
it is flight 968 to Istanbul
diverted to Manchester,
and you have to walk back.

Time leaks out of the clock
and scampers off sideways.

One woman
is three women
or no woman,
not necessarily
in that order.

You bastards knew all that,
didn't you?
You knew it all along,'
he said,
knocking over his beer.

'We tried to tell you,'
I said.
'We tried to tell you.'

STONE: STUDY NO 3

The prize that year
by unanimous acclaim
went to a man who proceeded as follows:
he bought a statue,
removed the head,
knocked off the limbs,
cut back the drapery,
then very carefully,
through months of work,
brought out the slab of undressed stone
hidden within the human figure.

After much thought,
he entitled it
'Stone: Study No 3'.

The judges praised the unflinching courage
with which he pursued his artistic vision,
'returning to the medium its lost power
to express its own innate integrity'.

Over their drinks the critics said
'questioning
at same time recreating
essential relationship artist-world,
transcending gulf
form-content artificial barriers,
external-internal,
remarkable synthesis process-product,
post-redeconstruction'.

He spent the prize money
on a sort of honeymoon
with a unicyclist
from Chipping Norton.

REVELATION

The time came
for God to speak.

As we waited,
clutching our tape recorders,
opinions were divided.
Would it be in
Hebrew, Aramaic, Greek, Latin?
Or would He use,
for example,
American, Russian or Mandarin?

The clock struck,
the clouds rolled back,
a light hurt our eyes,
and a great voice said
'Wa wa wa wa wa wa wa wa wa wa beep.'

Linguists are working on it.

SUZHOU: GUIDED TOUR

This is the Wu garden,
built during the Qing dynasty
by General Lu.
There are many old calligraphies
by the emperor Hu,
and an unusual Buddha.

This is the old Lu garden
built during the Yang dynasty
by General Qing.
Here are many calligraphies
by the emperor Wu,
and an unusual Buddha.

This is the pagoda
of the heavenly jade pool.
It has nine storeys,
and is built entirely of wood.

Here is an unusual garden,
built by the jade emperor
during the period
of the warring pagoda Buddhas.
There are many calligraphies,
and a heavenly old Wang.

This Wu
is an unusual calligraphy,
built entirely of jade wood
in the early part
of the Thing dynasty.
Note the upside-down Bagoda.

In this Lu
General Wang Gong Gong
built a jade palligraphy
in honour of
the unusual emperor Xu.

Wu hu hu.

PROFESSOR TURNER AND THE TEA-LADIES

When Professor Turner
lectured the tea-ladies
on quantum dynamics,
they were quite entranced.

All their lives
words had been urgent –
telling, scolding,
hurting, soothing.

Never before,
so strangely uplifting.
'Superposition of states ...
collapse of the wave-function ...
Bell-Aspect experiments ...
Einstein's objection
to action at a distance ...
thirteen-dimension
superstring theory ...'

Of *course* they didn't understand.
How wonderful
not to understand –
to be, for once,
overvalued.

With all the sweet mysteries
spinning in their heads,
out they skipped,
made wonderful tea.

ADVICE TO WOMEN

When you went off climbing mountains
I acted like most other women:
cultivated patience, wisdom,
sought consolation in reading poetry,
joined an ecological movement,
kept my eyes off calendars, clocks.

When you started collecting clocks,
piled them in the house in ticking mountains,
explained the secrets of their movement,
I smiled and nodded, in the way of women.
You said their chimes were cosmic poetry.
I held my tongue, with my female wisdom.

When you studied ancient wisdom,
told me time wasn't trapped in clocks,
and read me selections of Sanskrit poetry
sitting cross-legged on top of mountains,
I went along with it. Like many women
I could see these things brought change and movement.

When you took up dance and movement
and told me bodies were the whole of wisdom,
(especially men's, since compared with women
men have different biological clocks),
I didn't go and scream in the mountains,
but sought consolation in yet more poetry.

When you started writing poetry
I could see that this was a positive movement.
You deluged me with rhyming mountains
of paper. I loved your creative wisdom,
saw beauty in dustbins, cabbages, clocks,
sunsets and sandbags. God help women.

When you started collecting women,
saying they were needed for your poetry,
I burned your poems, smashed your clocks,
and joined the local anarchist movement.
You can stuff that ancient women's wisdom.
Faith in men doesn't move any mountains.

Advice to women: avoid movement;
keep clear of mountains; beware of clocks;
trust no one's wisdom; don't read poetry.

CONVERSATION NO 34: ABOUT THE HOTEL ROOM

Please have a green salad
and a glass of sparkling water
delivered quickly to my room.

It will be brought immediately, sir.

In my room
there is a lamp
which does not function.

I will attend to it at once, sir.

Also
the wallpaper pattern
is not comforting.

I am sorry to hear that, sir.
We cannot of course
make an immediate change,
but I will report your comments
to the Deputy Manager.

And further,
late in the evening,
memories of past deviations,
of confusions
and unaccomplished crossings
return to haunt me.

Perhaps, sir
one of the pay channels ...

In my room
I am there.
Can you understand?
I am there.
To be with oneself
in the same place
day and night –
Can you grasp what I am saying?

Sir, I must return to my duties.

EVERYTHING IS JOINED

Everything is joined.

Pick a blackberry,
and you are walking up steps
into a square
where your childhood
paused for a second.

Buy a newspaper,
and you are in a cafe
facing the door,
your cup half-empty, forgotten,
as your head spins with love.

Pick up the cup,
and you are playing the violin
very badly
in a dusty cellar.

How can you think of any one person,
or glance at your shoes,
or take a breath, even?

JUST WORDS

I hate you
I love you
you get on my nerves
you're destroying me
darling
don't leave me
it's your fault
you always
you never
darling
you never listen to me
don't listen to me
it's just words.

LAPSING INTO SANITY

Lapsing into sanity,
I feel some nostalgia
for the days
when the trees and I
talked at length about Plato;
when I kept the stars
in a mug by my bed,
and offered myself
on toast
to anyone hungry
who happened to be passing.

But I fear
there were other things
also.

In any event,
it is not good to look back.
I must dress properly
and work well at the office.

I LEARNT THE NAMES OF BUTTERFLIES

I learnt the names of butterflies,
but death was not moved.

I studied crystallography,
the curing of leather,
the history of the first world war.
Death stood firm.

I travelled,
learnt new languages,
mastered aircraft recognition.

Anaxander, Anaxagoras,
quanta and tailoring
did not hold off death.

I inspected the lists of the dynasties –
through all those blazing millennia,
death did not blink.

With more time,
I told him,
I could learn the clans of Scotland,
astrophysics, Swahili and tapestry-weaving,
the rules of piquet,
early steam-engines,
photosynthesis.

Shortly before the end
I re-read Jane Austen,
revised the flags of the world,
started on basic paper-making.

He waited at the end of the bed.

FROM THE TESTIMONY OF JOSEPH ERBER

They say we murdered
countless Jews.
That's not true.
That is simply
not true.
We counted them all
most carefully.

GOD THROWS A SIX

God throws a six.

He moves one.
The garden fiasco.

Two.
Altamira, Lascaux.

Three.
Attila, Genghiz and Tamburlane.

Four.
The E Major partita.

Five.
The dodo.

Six.
Dachau, Auschwitz, Sobibor.

God is due another throw.

He goes to the window
and stares out
for a long time.

PICNIC

Two old Jews
fell in love
on the way to the gas.
I mean it:
in love at first sight.
And they poured it all,
a lifetime of love,
into five minutes' talk,
touching hands
under the clubs,
under the guards' clubs.
Talk
about how
they would go on a picnic
in his little car,
and she would pack chicken
and salads
and honey cake
and strawberries and chocolates,
and he would bring champagne,
and they would sit
and smile
and look at the river
and talk,
new lovers.

That was the end.
They went through the doors
then.

MEMENTO, HOMO

From the creation
it has been there
between the stars.

And from our beginnings,
covering all our images,
all our stones and bones.

Swirled up by the wind
at Golgotha,
it stopped the voice
of the Good Thief.

Arthur at Avalon
saw in a vision
how it settled
on the Round Table,
little by little
choking all his bright chivalry.

As Charles stepped onto the scaffold,
the headsman
wiped a speck from his axe.

In Flanders,
carried on the summer breeze,
it coated
the lips and eyes of the dead.

Emperor,
Khan,
despot with the spear and the gold staff,
all lie in its dry arms.

Softly, softly,
it drifts between us,
into every crack,
every hollow of our love.

Invisible particles,
one a second,
burying the universe.

THE USUAL THINGS

The street is full of monstrous flashing signs
in ideograms you don't know how to read.
And underneath, a thousand foreign faces
all look the same.

But if you ever learn to read the signs,
you'll find the usual things: buy this, eat here,
give us your money, sell your soul, get sex.
The same as always.

And if you ever learn to read the faces,
you'll recognise confusion, rage, desire,
fatigue, resentment, courage, love, despair.
The usual things.

SUCH A CLEVER GHOST

It was a very clever ghost.
Always somewhere else.
If she looked under the bed
it was in the drawer with her blouses;
when she went to the drawer
it slipped behind the curtain
trailing a smell of lavender.

She wondered what colour it was.
It was the colour of all of her fears.
A sort of rainbow ghost.

It would move her things:
hide her keys,
take her photos,
and put them back in the same place,
but she could tell.

When she went into the garden,
it stared at her
from behind the shed.

She knew it would have her
in a sudden savage rush,
had felt its hot breath on her neck
often enough;
she knew it was poised.

She had taken precautions, of course:
never married
(he might be the ghost in disguise!);
didn't travel far;
counted her change, always;
refused to have repairs;
kept her little cat inside;
locked all doors and windows.

Such a clever ghost.
It stalked her all her life,
but held off, and held off
until one spring morning –
then a leap
at the old woman's throat.

She would not have been surprised
at the way it sat on her gravestone
swinging its legs
and laughing.

YOU COULD NOT KNOW

You could not know,
you could not begin to know,
as you came down to the place
where the trails joined,
as the wind
moved the sand grains along and back,
along and back, whispering,
covering the camel tracks in minutes,
you could not know for one instant
what had gone before,
or what awaited you;
and all your clever work
with the map and compass,
with the radio, and the noon observation
was for nothing,
as around you
from horizon to horizon
the rocks looked on.

VISITING DAY

You live in a parallel universe
in which, I understand,
spiders have a different role,
and things are tidier all round.

That is fine by me,
but answer me this:
do you all breathe on the left?
And if not,
how do you manage?

This morning
I was re-elected
deputy in charge of all containers.

Do you have fun at the office?

Do you have parades?
We have parades.
The words march past in columns of three
and I take the salute.

I told the nurse
that the ceiling was in the same place as my dressing-gown,
but he knew I was joking.

Green doesn't leak,
but red does.
Red leaks.

Did my mother tell you to come?

You know about the catherine wheels.
You know about the stars.
You know about the catherine wheel stars
don't you?
I told you about them last time.

How are the children?

WHEN THEY COME FOR YOU

When they come for you,
it is not as you expected.

One of them looks like the postman.
His shoes are worn.
The other is tough but decent-looking.
You give them a cup of tea.

Their questions are fair and reasonable.
There is no pressure.

Later, despite everything,
you remember them as good people.

WORDS IN A FOREIGN LANGUAGE

In your room
there is a carpet
with thirty-two squares
of the finest silk.

In the squares: birds,
orange trees and roses;
in the heart of one rose,
if you look carefully,
a door.

Through the door
a horse standing,
saddled and bridled.

You ride gently,
not hurrying,
as far as a bridge
where there is a boat.

At the mouth of the river
a three-master.

You cross oceans,
weather storms;
at last, a landfall
where you are welcomed
with songs and garlands.

Hard, now,
to remember your children's names
and the touch of their hands –
like words in a foreign language.

A COUPLE OF ADJECTIVES

'A couple of adjectives
now and then
never hurt anyone,'
said my friend the poet.
'I can take them
or leave them alone.'

Look at him now,
his thesaurus
tilted to his lips,
sprawling
in the clamorous,
coruscating,
many-textured,
odoriferous,
indifferent
gutter.

ME AND THE PAGE

It's just me and the page.

Eyeball to eyeball.

The first to blink loses.

That blank
poker-faced
bastard.

Not a flicker.

I think it's winning.

ATMOSPHERIC POEM

Against a lowering eastern sky
full of the threat
of the year's death
the leafless trees stand
stark, vigilant
like frontier guards
on some..
I'm getting bored
you write the rest.

AUTOGRAPH

You asked for my autograph.

Behind you
all your life and loves
hidden, like an army,
in dead ground,
and mine behind me,
and the two of us
meeting for the first and last time,
neutrals,
parlying under a white flag.

The scrap of paper signed,
we march away
in opposite directions.

CARPE SOMETHING

One's reach, you say,
should far exceed one's grasp.
I'm with you there.

My arms stretch out
towards a hundred objects of desire.

I keep my eyes
fixed on the unclimbed peaks,
the record marathon,
the book that sets the world on fire,
the knighthood offered and declined,
the Nobel Prize.

One's grasp:
that's where the problem lies.
Wrenching my gaze
back from the Oscar and the Oxford Chair,
I clasp
my mug of instant coffee, stare
into the mirror at my thinning hair.

FROM CATULLUS: ‘VIVAMUS, MEA LESBIA’

Time for living,
Lesbia,
time now for loving.
Pay no attention
to old men’s carping.
Suns can go down, and
come back in the morning,
but when our little light
has once finished burning,
there’s one long night
for ever
for sleeping.

LILLAZ

1

The mountain is what it is.
The landscape fits together without a join.
There are the right number of trees.
The rocks are where they are.
The slope falls just so.

Marmot-holes,
ibex-tracks,
butterflies,
rhododendrons,
dust and scree
all have their places.

Words have no power here.
The mountain will accept little from us:
a small house grown into the hillside,
a low cairn carefully built.

2

Under a rock
that no one has looked at
insects are busy;
in a fold of ground
where nobody walks
there are gentians;
hidden in a cleft
a stream falls.

Night comes;
there are stars in the water.
Light that set out
before our world was conceived.

A stone settles in the streambed.
In the time it takes to settle
we are born and gone.

A star fades a little
and the stream and the stone are past.

3

Here
on the last day
– a long last day
with the earth spinning slowly now
so far from the sun –
here,
when the leaves fall for the last time,
each leaf will fall in its place
(here there are no wrong places);
ibex
will fold their legs under them,
quietly, quietly,
with a last whistle of breath;
birds will perch,
gentians fade,
for the last time;
butterflies
that no one has looked at
will settle forever.

On the last day,
so many things that we have not done
will not now be done.

But here,
peacefully,
at the right time,
rivers will freeze;
there will be no more wind;
clouds will stand still;
no more stones will fall;
the last light
will drain for ever
from the evening hills.

LOST IN TRANSLATION

This poem has been translated
from a language
that is no longer spoken,
in order to give it
a wider readership.
Inevitably
it has lost something
in the process:
the original is written
in hendecasyllables
with a complex internal rhyme scheme,
and is about something completely different.